Waxworks

FRIEDA HUGHES

Waxworks

HarperCollins*Publishers*

HarperCollins books may be purchased for educational,
business, or sales promotional use. For information, please
write: Special Markets Department, HarperCollins Publishers
Inc., 10 East 53rd Street, New York, NY 10022.

Acknowledgements are due to the editors of the following
publications in which some of these poems first appeared:
The Spectator: 'Dr. Crippen'
Thumbscrew: 'Malchus'
The Tatler: 'Cinderella'

Originally published in Great Britain in 2002 by Bloodaxe
Books Ltd.

FIRST EDITION

Library of Congress Cataloging-in-Publication Data is available
upon request.

ISBN 0-06-001269-2

03 04 05 06 07 ❖ / PHX 10 9 8 7 6 5 4 3 2 1

For Laszlo, with love

CONTENTS

Waxworks

Medusa

She is the gypsy
Whose young have rooted
In the very flesh of her scalp.

Her eyes are drill-holes where
Your senses spin, and you are stone
Even as you stand before her.

She opens her lips to speak,
And have you believe.
She has more tongues to deceive

Than you can deafen your ears to.
If you could look away, the voices
From the heads of her vipers

Would be heard to argue.
If you could look away,
The pedestals of your feet might move.

If you could look away,
The song from the cathedral of her mouth
Would fall to the floor like a lie.

1

Madame Tussaud

Marie Grosholtz has been shopping.
Among the Louis Vuitton handbags
She found Dr Crippen,
His moustache like a zipper
Fixing his lips together.

She uncovered Durga, cradling her corpses
In the discounted section
Of the Army and Navy,
Nails like penknives, blunted
By cutting Berberis for wreaths.

She met Thor in his bear-paw slippers
Commiserating with Loki
Over a vodka and tonic in a London club.
And outside, Houdini, swinging from a street-lamp
Screaming for a key to his padlock.

Already a collector of heads
For her library of faces,
She is putting together a family,
Gathering up the possibilities
And taking them home in effigy.

*

She is looking for fingers to fit
The two wedding-bands from her dead father's
First marriage to her dead mother.
He'd thought to have them cut in two,
Half each of each for Marie and her brother.

He'd thought a friend would care
For his two rings, and his two children
Who cried out when he died
To keep his last two pieces uncut,
When everything else had been torn up.

But Herse had already looked
In the baby's basket,
And was made mad. She returned the rings
With a curse for not being divided
As a father's last wish, by her little saw.

With other wishes for his children
Left undone, this was the only one
When stopped, would leave them something whole.
Marie thinks Sisyphus will do,
Or Samson, or Zeus, or Thor.

She has worked out their shapes,
And boiled their actions and vanities
Into their features. She will see how they fit;
When sculpted in wax
Her likeness sits among them.

She'll make a mould of Herse too,
When Herse has thrown herself from the top
Of the Acropolis. She'll paint on a face.
If her work be collecting biographies,
Then madness has its place.

Pandora

What has she got in her box
But photographs. Starched with age,
Imprinted with hands and faces
Browning as if tanned,
And smiling mouths, unrelated
By blood or friendship.

She never looks,
She knows them exactly
For their features. There is a dead mother
She never met, whose children
Are disembodied from their memories
By the box-lock and Pandora's grasp.

There is a father too, dead now, whose flesh
Is ashes even while his likenesses
Outlive him. Mostly unseen, uncopied,
Or unsent to his children. Pandora keeps
The charred package of his body
Separate from his photographs.

One day she may scatter the first in the fields,
But will she ever release the second?
Should she cast out her collection
She would cast out the world's evil –
All that filled her with asperity,
All that gave her purpose.

Maybe it has been so long now
That she and the box are interchangeable.
If the box were emptied
She would rattle like an empty tin
With one thing left in for alms,
And if at last she spoke,

That one thing left is hope.

Damocles

Damocles has been advising his sister
Against her three children.
She has confided in him
The injustice she feels
At being questioned.

Her brother answers.
His words describe her rights in keeping
What the children understood was theirs,
When she could not detach herself
From her apparent wrongs.

But she cannot convince them
Of her innocence, even
With the knives he has given her
To defend her protestations of truth.
Her sharpened edges divorce them.

Like dogs that cannot be unbeaten,
They've gone. They no longer want
What she warranted was theirs,
It frees them from hope
That she'll keep the promise she broke.

Nor is her secret safe,
She will sink with the weight of it.
And Damocles sees at last, the sword,
Hung above his shoulder-blades
By a thread from a horsetail

In the head of his sister.

Medea

When Medea's eyes observed Jason
Floundering among the Argonauts
For the Golden Fleece,
She knew she had the means
By which to marry him.

She could make the end of effort,
Of sweat and longing,
Seem as close as the fingers
On her out-held hand, if only,
If only he would hold it

And make promises. She gave him
The ointment to make bulls blind
And sang the song of persuasion
That stupefied dragons,
Until he had the sheepskin

Dangling from his two fists,
Dripping lanolin and ore.
Only to find it was bedding
For his two brats, and she,
The mother-to-be.

Jason feared this woman;
This sharpened axe
With an eye for the thing he carried
Between his thighs, and the gap
On her ring finger.

He thought he would cast her
Out to sea in a boat,
To be carried off by the current
So he could imagine her better,
Happier elsewhere. Begun again.

But she was forged from stock of steel;
Mother of metal, father
Unreasoning of foreigners,
Ploughing their bodies
Into fields for the birds.

She could not uproot
Her wish to be his wife, her very will
Demanded he adore her. She wanted
To obviate his speech and cast
His words of protest to the wind

Like broken pigeons. When Jason loved elsewhere,
While Medea still dragged in the shackles
She wished to bind him with,
All reason abandoned her
As he had.

She dangled her end like a rope,
From which she might hang
If he did not attend her
Frequently, for the face of it,
Among friends,

Keeping up appearances.
Until he lay down one day,
Too tired with trying
To unpick her like a deadly orchid
From his branches, and died.

Now she severed the children
From their attachment, with a knife
That looked like a pen
In the hand of a lawyer.
She did not care they could not

Be put back later, to crawl
Wriggling into their cold skins
To be hers again, as if donning a tunic.
Without them there would be nothing
To show she was less-loved or the loser.

Far cleverer this, than a poison gown
For his new bride, and her own death.
Or an ending to it;
Forgive and goodbye,
And move on.

Her brother beware,
Lest she descry
That he was the one overheard
Telling her story,
And be cut into pieces.

Burke and Hare

Burke, being penniless,
Tried to work out
Who would put up the least resistance
If he borrowed from them.

It occurred to him
With sudden clarity of vision,
That those who would not complain
Were those who could not talk.

And the dumbest of them all
Were the dead.
He could dig up each ended life
And render it with meaning.

He could write out its diaries
And dismember its intention
In his own words,
So to speak.

He could sell it then, as newly anointed
For vivisection. His work
Was all in the discovery,
In the presentation,

And his part done,
He would start looking for another one.
Funerals were thin on the ground
When he met Hare,

Who kept a household for trolls
And travellers, and an idea
For earning a penny or two
From their blood and history,

Each one different for the slab,
For the butcher's table,
As one by one
They died.

But in the end, not fast enough
For Burke and his new friend.
They couldn't wait for the cadaver
So now, the corpses were fresh

From a drunken cup
And the feathers of a pillow.
And someone was recognised
As too recently alive.

Then Burke himself, was sold on to die,
And Hare counted the most
He'd ever made for the trade,
In his days left.

Imprisoned in the room of his head
All he could see was the price
Per passer-by. He must have wept
To watch so much money walking.

Circe

In the beginning, the child
Whose bandied legs became
The stalks on which you stand,
Played with a stick.

The stick in your hand
Was made magic by the grip
Of your fingers, as if it was
Conducting for music.

But music did not play
The way the creatures did.
You found your childish toys
In the men you changed.

A bored movement made a goat
From the man who cut wood
Who laid his head in your lap,
Glad for a girl's thighs.

And the man who killed chickens
For your mother's table became the dog
Whose mouth of bloodied feathers
Slept at your bedside.

And your mother's lover
Walked out one afternoon,
Left his shoes to come back for
As if he would be back soon.

And a weeping rat
Scuttled the house
Searching the floor for its footwear,
Driven on by your laugh.

Now your stalks dance
To the faces of men, mooning
Beyond the stage-end.
You swing hip over knee

To stretch an ankle
And one man is a humping camel.
Your breasts shake free
From their silver cups,

Another man shrivels up
Until his ferret-face
Is all that hangs over
His dropped collar.

You no longer need a wand
To make animals of men,
Your body has become
The thing that makes men beasts.

Rasputin

He's selling God, you can buy the book;
Six dollars a bible. He sells life insurance
On the side and can do a deal
On a car for the cash and a ride.

His wife is pregnant again – each child
By a stranger, he says to the girls
Who want to understand his vast kindness
In taking on another man's burden.

If they looked a little closer they'd see
His face on each of the three, bastards
By rumour only, his wife undone
And left when he found another one.

But his eyes like pointy spears, darting out
From their almond greens, are looking
For anyone who won't ask questions
And move him on. What he has seen

Are the voids that women carry; their wounds
Wanting to be stopped up and gagged.
'Come sin with me,' he tells them,
'And my forgiveness will set you free.'

'God is embedded bodily, as if I have
Been marked out by the gift
Of his most powerful blessing and made
Immortal. My hands are magic.'

And his hands performed. They took
Houses, cars and chequebooks.
The old and the infirm came to him,
Their powers of attorney flapping

Like winter cloaks, eager to be given
To a man who promised warmth
In return for their investment.
When, one by one, cast out as empty,

The men and women stood up in only
The emperor's new clothes, they discovered
He'd been poisoned once for fraud, and lived,
As if God acknowledged his apology.

So this time they shot him.

Narcissus

It was only a look
For a second, made to drink
And see the face before me,
Upon me. To disgrace
All other noses, their slope
None as quick as mine.

I marvel at its perfect point
Between the mounds
Of my cheekbones. The space between
My face and my face
Is a thing that keeps me
Too far from it. I should

Drown to be near enough.
Two eyes fix my own
Like rods of polished steel, brow to brow.
I wonder at them, wondering at me.
There is no flaw that I can see
As I trace the liquid of

Each perfect feature, of myself.
I am caught up in my search,
In disbelief, and rooted.
Here I will flower.

Samson

Delilah thought her scissors would get him.
That he would lie in her arms, bewitched,
Then sleep, his long black hair
Shorn to the scalp of his magic.

She thought his muscles would waste
And weaken. That the pillars of his building
Would fall beneath the weight
Of her womanhood.

She imagined that his body, cut off
From what made it most beautiful
Would shrivel at its own ugliness,
Lost, without its lion's mane.

She had studied herself and seen
The root of her own vanity. She thought
His would be the same. That once uglied,
He would stay.

She took each of his tresses
And felled them. On the floor,
His tangles writhed and died, divested
Of the head that gave them purpose.

Samson woke from the soft nest
Of her thighs. His eyes
Took in everything. She smiled
And waited for him to topple.

'My weakness,' he said, stepping over
What had once adorned him, 'was you.
But you have severed me from your lap
With your sharp edges, and now I am free.'

17

Sibyl

Sibyl and Herophile are playing chess.
They have before them
All the pieces they need
To work out a conclusion.

But each is wise to consequence;
Each has an eye
On the next move
In the head of the other.

Herophile had promised action
Based on a letter from
Someone, dead now. But Sibyl saw
Each undertaking made as straw

In the fire of Herophile's
Other intentions, blazing and gone
As wind-blown ash
Withers, and is worthless.

Now Herophile swears an oath
That the past, which Sibyl sees
Playing behind Herophile's cornea
As if her eye were the keyhole,

Is only conjecture.
Whereas she can clearly discern
Sibyl's purpose as being
One of argument and delay,

When Sibyl only wants to position
Her first piece, but Herophile
Is arguing and delaying, it being
Her move.

For as the game is not begun,
Neither is it won.
But stagnant, waiting, unended,
Always, always.

Rumpelstiltskin

Rumpelstiltskin wants a child.
Crumpled in on his face,
Hunchbacked and trailing his ears,
He knows there isn't a woman alive
Who would lie down for him.

Once he spun gold from hay
For a workman's daughter,
Three times, to marry her off
To a king who coveted her fingers,
All for the price of an infant.

Just for a game, to stop up her wail of protest
When he came to collect,
She must guess his name, he said,
And he would forgive the debt.
He limped off laughing, to wait.

But she caught him out; he was seen
Applauding himself as Rumpelstiltskin.
It took him years to unpick
His right foot from the earth
Into which his fury propelled it.

Rumpelstiltskin wants a child,
He is too old to adopt, even as a non-smoker
Working from home. He could teach it
To spin gold from straw
But no one wants his skill anymore.

He is searching hospital bins for anything
With life left in. He can make
A silk purse from a sow's ear, a clutch bag
From a severed hand, or a descendant
From a cut-out ovary.

Thor

He was tempted with love tokens,
He was fed morsels that bewitched the palate,
He was sung to by a voice
From the throat of one of

God's most blessed instruments,
And for a moment
He put down his hammer and shield
And thought of peace.

He unstrapped his sword
And unbuckled his helmet,
And washed off the skin-oil of battle
While his woman watched.

It was as his head
Was bent over the basin
That she thrust the skewer
Through the cartilage of his nose.

He reared up in anger,
And she slipped a brass ring
Through the wound.
She attached a chain.

Each time he moved
Or swung his head,
The pain would floor him.
He became stationary.

His bulk huddled in shame;
He drew his bearskin
So tight around, he was
Unrecognised.

She sang to torment him,
Laughing. Her first notes
Would take hold of his feet
In their bear-paw slippers

And make them prance to her music.
'Come and see!' she sang,
As he was compelled to dance,
'Come and see my husband.'

Sisyphus

Dead, she is piled on his back
For the river crossing.

Before, he rolled his stone
Up the mountain while
His wife watched. And then
They watched it roll down again.
It defied him. Now he is
Carrying his wife's carcass.

He reaches the river bank. Mud
Is thick at his ankles.
Her body stinks from
The buckle of his shoulders
But the gathered crowd
Will not land him. They stand,
Bank-stuck, their words
Sharp like swords, and hold him off.

Slowly, current tugging at his
Bent knees, he turns. Slowly,
He wades back. But they are
Waiting there too, tongues pointed
Like knives. And his wife
Is weighing heavy for her burial.

He turns again.

Houdini

Houdini hangs like a swinging peach,
Ropes twisted and knotting,
Chains padlocked, and limbs caught up
In a foetal crouch.

He is convinced that his sister
Is the mistress of his misfortune
Because his ties were fastened
By his stepmother's fingers,

And he wants to find a goat
He can scape for the fault
He wishes to relieve his stepmother of,
So she won't cast him off like a stitch.

He watched his sister cut free
When she accepted the umbilical scissors
In her stepmother's voice
And thorny embrace,

Not pretending any more
That the blades of severance
Were not hidden in every welcome,
Because she wore her mother's face.

But Houdini, with a look like his father's,
Knew he'd been favoured. So the knots
That grind his flesh, and the padlocks
That staple his chains, madden him now.

He will hang for as long as it takes
To let his stepmother go, and know
She would always have done what she did
And hidden it, just the same.

Simeon

He's dying up there, on his feet for his audience,
Speaking for God. You make him work
For your stolen hour,
He holds it like mud in his hands.

As his mouth moves, his eyes
Scrabble back into his head behind
His occipital arches, like beetles
Wanting priest-holes to hide in.

Only his unstuck tongue
Keeps flapping like an open gate,
All his cattle escaping; his words
Leggily stumbling from ear to ear.

Your questions like waving arms
Stagger the beasts, clod-hopped and craven,
To the four corners of the room
Where they fall, and heap mutely.

Skin-wrapped and smarter you have
Not heard arrogance or idiot, but youth,
Ridiculed beneath your practice,
As caught as you, in your hour,

Knowing he has a while to wait
For Jesus.

Malchus

Malchus is hopping mad for his ear.
He has just seen the very man
Who might know the right stitch
To re-fix it, and give it life,
Carried off by soldiers and Pharisees.
The disciple who severed it, follows them,
Dragging his sword.

Malchus collects his flap of curling flesh
And, holding his palm up against
The hole in the side of his head
To stop the air whistling in it,
He hurries off for a place in the crowd
Who wait for Jesus. It is he, who cries out
'Get down, get down, King of the Jews,

If God is your father, how can he
See you dangle like meat, by nails in your palms
And not set you free?
Demand a miracle!' Jesus just smiles.
Malchus, hand in his pocket, begins to pray.
If Jesus is saved, he will
Pull out his ear and be waiting.

Lady Macbeth

Her careful hands, each
As big as a small horse,
Have dealt with her burden.
Despatched it, even.

'Your sucklings will not feed
At my breast,' she cries,
And cuts out his pig from the herd
Where his children are fed.

She will be a widow, first,
Before ever he
Gathers up his young
And runs.

Cinderella

Cinderella climbs from the dishwasher.
She has picked the last scrap
Of her stepmother's linguini
From the open pores
Of the metal drum.

With her hands in the ashes
Of the grate in which hope smoulders,
She is doubtful of rescue by her prince
And a golden slipper. She decides
To go it alone and leave home.

It will free her from waiting
At her stepmother's hearth
For a man wielding a shoe and a scrotum,
While her sisters toss her
Fish heads and bones.

She has choices now, and if age
Should outweigh her womanhood
Before she finds a husband,
She'll use a cell donor for the extra
Chromosomes, or be cloned.

Jezebel

She must imprint him,
She is screaming at the door
To be let in.

One time, she must have him.
Maybe twice, to tattoo his elements
To her uneventful skin.

His stain on the folds of her membrane,
Her Turin shroud,
Could lose him his name.

Added to the others,
He will flesh her out. She is nothing
Except through her lovers.

Is he ever going to let her in?

*

Down on her luck,
Jezebel is counting her conquests.
Unknown to them
They have fallen.
She is thinking of selling them off.

She combs her hair and
Applies rouge. Some of them
Are women.

*

Jezebel's head
Has been severed
By a cartwheel. It rolls off,
Followed by dogs and children.

Her body will pack
Into a small bag.
Every broken bone,
Another hinge.

'Am I not beautiful?' she cries,
Her last sentence whispered
From her blunt neck-end
Like the whistle of a hollow reed.

A passing woman bends over the open mouth
And fills it with dirt.
'Quiet, now,' she says,
'Or someone will hear you.'

Loki

Loki is trawling the room
For someone he recognises
To pay his bar bill. Anyone wise
Looks away, lest he notice

A moment of weakness.
He can almost smell it out.
Feel good for cash, and
He'll go away. Better the beggar you know.

If he sits on the arm of the couch
Beside the sniffers of coke, and smiles,
They will surely include him
On their next line.

There is nothing like a little sin
To encourage the welcome of converts.
If they will only acknowledge him,
He will make them feel like kings.

He keeps their names held tight,
Up against the glass of his next drink.
Each name is a talisman,
Turned like a key in the ears of strangers.

If he could find a woman to sleep with,
She might take him home.
For a bed and his cab-ride
He will stay the night.

He would move in for a meal.
But the body he sells
Hasn't seen a weight for a while,
And the coke and the booze and the fictitious smile

Are wearing him thin.
Now pity is what pays for him.
For a beer he will number
The jobs he can't get, for a vodka

He'll tell you how others are first
For the flat he can't rent,
So he's left behind,
Still sleeps in a tent,

And those friends he ignored
Are much harder won.
Then he'll ask for his cab fare
Because while talking to you

The last bus has gone.

Judas

Judas didn't start out
By looking for the son of God.

When he was young
He had hopes for himself.
He measured his width
Against the shoulders of other men,

He judged his stature
Against their consequence,
He recorded his thoughts in the belief
That his brilliance would be recognised.

Until he realised
No one was listening,
They had already found
The man they wanted to follow.

Needing company, he joined himself up
With the acolytes. But having lost his voice
Because a man unheard
Makes no sound,

He bided his time,
And his time came.
He sent out a subtle breath,
Barely there, but for the odour

Of his last meal. In it
He hid the whisper that the man
Was an impostor,
Not a king in the making.

When his whisper was brought back to him
As a shout in the mouths of others,
No one remembered
Where their ears had first detected it,

And he stood tall in the defence
Of the man he had damned,
Thereby pointing him out
For an ending.

The man who had reached out to Judas
And taken him in, was nailed up
By the palms of his hands, to die.
The crowds mourned, and again

Judas was ignored. Suddenly,
He raised his head and cried;
'But wait, mourn with me, for I
Was his dearest, closest friend.'

'To demonstrate my authenticity,
Watch me damn his disciples
And know me then,
For my impartiality.'

Malvolio

Malvolio is made mad. Letters
Have undone him before, but now
He sits to write his own.
His yellow-stockinged legs incline
Cross-gartered beneath his desk,
Like sour rain-sticks, pouring,
While his fingers itch.

His sister's honour, he writes,
Is central to her core. He knows
She would never lie or steal, but,
Having appeared to do so,
Only did because her probity
Was somewhat in question.
We must know it is ourselves at fault.

Had we not seen it, his sister
Would have proved us wrong.

He seals his note and smiles,
As letters from the one he loves
Have made him do, in spite
Of spite. He may send
A birthday card with this, to show
Discussion at an end, and truth
Be so deluded.

Hippolytus

Son of an Amazon,
He found himself mothered elsewhere
When his father remarried.
But Phaedra did not have
That blood-lock that must stop
Her wanting him.
She was wanton in her efforts
To bed her new son.
His silence damned him,
As speech would damn his father.
'You must marry!' Theramene cried,
'And your new wife
Will be the flint from which
Your mother's glances fall.' But he was
Not gladdened by this.
'Each female form I think complete,
Each eye, the hair,
The nose, the feet,
Reminds me that I see the witch
In every rising breast, beneath
Each clasp of hands.
The fear that cripples me,
Is how my bride will be
Upon our wedding night;
That I will have chosen
A Phaedra-monster of my own,
Who will betray me
As my father is betrayed.
Better be alone
And take what comes.'

Durga

Durga's four arms embrace
As much as no longer struggles.
Her red palms are pitiless
In their acquisition of anything
Devoid of the breath to protest.

Born as a ball of steel,
She was rolled in her mother's mouth
And spat into a furrow,
Where her father ploughed her in
Expecting her to flower. Now

She prays at her father's rectangle,
To his withered wreaths; she can't love his bones
Because he was ash when she dug him in
And rain has made mud of him.
On the kitchen wall, two foxhounds

Have replaced themselves in photographs
For twenty years since they died.
Home now and hung, she won't
Keep another alive to be tempted
By a neighbour's scraps.

On the stairs, a big-buttocked water buffalo
Displays his meat in a painting.
His life as a pet dogged him until
His legs crumpled at last beneath his beef,
And she buried him, all a ton,

In a hole in the desert.
His horns on a stone mark his bones,
But his flesh has escaped her in pieces,
Eaten up by ants and maggots,
Becoming winged and flying off.

Her husband is boxed in the bedroom.
She thinks he belongs to her now,
But it was nothing to give her
The bag of gravel he became in the furnace,
Devoid of him and empty of argument.

She lays wreaths at his parents' headstone
And sends flowers to his late wife,
Her spite as fresh as her carnations
For those other features; inflection and fingers
Remembered in the woman's daughter. Her petals betray.

The illusion of care with each thoughtful bouquet
Is pointless to a buried husk, but she'll have
The skull for a bead when no one is looking;
A string through the ear holes, its chin
Warmed on the skin of her breastplate.

The bodies pile up to be mourned and pitied,
Some incinerated. She buys another wreath,
She sends another card, she claims ownership
And a pair of earrings after
The sudden stoppage of blood and laugher.

The living go on without her.

Romulus and Remus

Romulus and Remus
Were born to be kings once.
Mars had impregnated their mother
Even as she tended
Vesta's fire, but being sons
Of the daughter
Of a fallen king,
They were tossed into the Tiber
To sink in a trough.

Fed by a wolf and a woodpecker
When they came to rest by the fig tree,
They were going to live.

Found by Faustulus,
They were going
To learn to talk.

Fathered by Mars
They were going
To be unbeatable.

Old enough to fight
They won the throne back
For their fallen king,
And for themselves
They built a city.
Romulus called out
For strays to fill it with,

The lost and the fugitive,
The seekers of asylum,
But mostly men. Remus knew
They needed women,
Even though he didn't want one.
He set up a party
For the Sabines, and stole
Their wives and daughters.

Now their government was moulded
And all its parts in place.
Romulus made up a wall
With his iron will
To keep his people in.

Remus couldn't see
The sense of it, it did not embody
The intent of others.
To prove its futility
He cleared it in a single bound
And became dangerous.

Romulus, blinded by autocracy,
Severed his brother from
His principles, and declared that anyone
Who disagreed, should die.
If he had wanted a democracy,
He would have asked them.

Merlin

Merlin gazes upon the sea of manuscripts
Laid out in blocks
Like the fallen wall of a building;
A life's thought
Written on something weighing nothing
And sold by the ton,
Taking up a whole floor.
He believes that no one
Has an eye like him.
He believes that no one
Notices a missing thing.
His quick fingers appear to make absent
A notebook whose conclusions
You'll never reach again.
They will become as doubtful
As the memory that you saw the book,
There, on the floor, among others,
As if it had not already been taken.
But still you look. Merlin, laughing,
Leaves his briefcase for you.
You open it, arguing that a quick search
Will eliminate that unlikeliness.
Merlin knows this, his spell is doubt.
Now your remembered hands
Are uncertain that they touched,
Turned over and replaced
The very thing you touched,
Turned over and replaced.
Doubt planted, Merlin thinks
He is safe.

Job

When Job was a woman,
God thought she was perfect.

He watched over her when,
As a girl, she took her first
Faltering steps into his church,
Gazed upon the crowd
That worshipped him,
And knew she must belong.

He watched her progress as
She decided to do
Everything that was right.
Her determination was born strong
In her young heart
And he had great hope for her.

Satan begged to differ.
He did not send boils this time,
His tests of endurance
Were more subtle now.
He sent a beggar with blackened fingers
Who reached out and found money.
He sent the maimed and the sick
To have their wounds bound,
Their faces washed
And their faeces wiped away.

He sent a widower to make
The woman his wife,
Whose infants she mothered.
The roses were planted, and,
If she were collecting grievances
God could not see it in the face
She held up to him on Sunday,
Like a clean plate, for his blessing.

When God took her husband
Satan gave her fair warning,
She got his will in place.
From the look on her face
Even God thought
She was sorry to lose him.
In her grief she was seen
To be akin to God; a heroine.

The father wrote his wishes
As his reason for his will,
He died believing that
His children would receive
Those things of his
He wanted them to have.
Their father's words, Job swore,
Were sacrosanct. For a year
She polished them brightly,
Holding them up to the light
So the children could see
Their birthright shining.

'Never think that I would take
Your share from you for money's sake;
You shall have it now,'
She said at last.
With her promise
Still fresh in her mouth,
Still wet with ink
In the writing,
She kept
Almost everything.

God watched her in church.
He couldn't fathom it;
How could she do what she did
And pray?
He called to her in dreams,
But she ignored him.
He reasoned with her in
Her waking hours, speaking
Through the mouth of a crow
In her conscience, but she
Sent for a gunman to shoot it
And Satan gave her the bullet.

Now God knew there was
No hope.
Every one of his creatures
Had its price.

Nebuchadnezzar

Nebuchadnezzar has built a temple
Fit for ministers and kings.
He has gathered together the gold
From friends and relatives,
But mostly from his subjects
For the cost of its assembly. Its dome
Rises from the dirt, as bald
And bleached as an empty cranium.
All they must do is pay to see it, and queue.

Inside, he has erected his idol,
His two-headed behemoth,
For all worship, for all races,
For both sexes, pleasing no one.
Undistinguished, indeterminate,
The figure reclines in obeisance to its maker.
Sexed, but sexless, it is missing fingers and features
With which to identify itself. Around it
Are built vestibules to prayer and science,

To talk, to other idols, to silence
And the inner sanctums of the body.
Recorded, filmed, piped through speakers,
Unreeled on screen, nothing to offend the children
Dragging at the loose ends of the votaries
Who wait in turn to pay homage,
Wanting communion, meant to applaud;
The temple worthless unless
The crowds are fully crowding.

Nebuchadnezzar has made from gold
A thing that once yearly must consume
Its own weight in the same metal.
Unable to satisfy its aimless appetite
The sacrifices and offerings cease.
The dome-idol shrivels from lack of conviction.
The occiput in which it sat, pointlessly,
Flakes in the sun. It would have been better
Left empty until purpose found it.

Its coronet of nails protrude,
That could not pin down
The little thoughts that filled it,
Better off not echoing to the sounds
Of the false prophets that inhabited
Its inner ear. Better off
As its white reaches begin
To scumble and peel, succumbing
To the elements.

The acrobats and musicians
Go home without an audience. Nebuchadnezzar
Holds an auction for the innards.
The success of the sale
Is not reported. The cost
Of the upkeep of the empty skull-top
Is not publicised. Nebuchadnezzar's temple
Has become his tower of Babel
Since accounts of his triumph are now told
In sixteen different languages,
All of them English, none of which includes
The name of his achievement.

Sweeney Todd

All the lies lined up as little pies
And somewhere, a fingernail.

If he makes you pay first
For a shave and a cut of hair,

Have a guess that his slipped razor
Will have severed your jugular

Even as the barber's chair
Tilts you into his meat factory.

You will be reshaped
And pastry baked.

You will feed dozens
From his bakery window,

And one of us is going to find
Your lost fingertip, like a toy in a lucky dip,

Or a pudding sixpence among the raisins
Wanting to break teeth.

Someone will pick out the oddity
And know it for belonging to a body,

A bit of finger-gristle
Clinging to its last message

Like a leftover.

Salome

Salome sways with her drink.
It is many years
Since the movement of her hips
Brought her the head
Of John the Baptist.

She has been a headhunter
Ever since, but those who knew her
Could not swim in the river of blood
At her ankles,
From another sacrifice.

Such a joke, to have
A head for a dance
As a gift. To know
A life was snatched like a pearl
So she could enjoy

The dead shell in which
The brain sagged. And all
The words the head spoke
Of her pointlessness,
Now silent in its pointless mouth,

Its windpipe ending
At the tin of the plate
On which it rests.
The head smiles to itself,
Even though its odour precedes it,
It still looks better than she does.

Vlad the Impaler

I love to see the little trees,
Their branches cut, their barbs
Like sharpened spears, be blunted
By adorning heads.
Apple-bobbing fleshy balls,
With eyes a-popping, and ears
To give a starling purchase
Where once were twigs.

And see my arch of bones;
A tangled thing of limbs
As stripped and bare as crows can make,
And leading off, my avenue of stakes
Rise tall above a man,
Each topped off by a face in which
Two puddles for a thirsty beak
Were irises, till thirst was quenched
And holes began.

And here, I roll your children's heads,
Orifices fit for fingers,
Jaws wired for silence,
And play skittles with their arms and legs.

Morgan Le Fey

Morgan's magic had already stripped
Fifteen years from the skin of her face
By the time she met Merlin. She was working
On the stasis of flesh
For the foreseeable future,
And had buried her birth certificate.

Merlin, growing backwards,
Thought he'd met his mate
And married her.

Together, they were going to launch themselves,
They would be celebrities.
She would dance and sing
And remain beautiful, invisibly ageing
Beneath the bottled features
She uncorked daily and poured
Into her palms for application.
He would be erudite and write
Music for her, the strings of his guitar
Plucking out the notes, even as they
Hurtled from her throat.

They collected new friends –
Only ones known well enough to perform
As ladder rungs for Morgan's pretty feet
Would do, her heels like thorns.

But every day they began again, unrecognised,
Having got nowhere, like Sisyphus
Looking up at his mountain. Morgan,
Promising to dance a little faster,
Persuaded Merlin to invest
In stage-time, a backing band,
A photographer and dancemaster.

But the audience still eluded her.
Another little drink and she thought
She'd get them tomorrow. Another little sip
And she could polish the idea
Until it dazzled.

Waking one morning, head
As clogged as a drain, Morgan saw Merlin
Lying like dross in the tangled sheets.
She gazed down at his sleeping buttocks,
His open jaw and unconscious snore,
She examined his impoverished chequebook
And felt cheated. Leaving a love letter,
She boarded a plane for Morocco
And left him.
Magic, she thought, was all very well
When it got you somewhere.

Scarlet with rage and remonstrating
With the effigy of Morgan
That he kept in his head,
As if she might suddenly come to life
And love him, Merlin festered and boiled.

If only he could spoon her out of his cranium,
Dead, or ended, it didn't matter.
If only he could untie
Her long black hair from the ligature at his neck,
If only he could unpick her fingernails
Buried up to the first knuckle,
From the small of his back,
If only he could unstick her wet tongue
From the end of his penis,
If only he could expel the sound of her last laugh
From the membrane in his ear
Which now so betrayed him,
In time, he would be free.

Merlin is counting down time by its known units,
Devising new ways to mathematically divert himself.
He is sloughing off his wife like scales
To find new skin. He is counting the scales.
He counts the parasites on each of the scales.
He counts the mites on each of the parasites.
He counts the legs on each of the mites on each of the parasites.

Morgan ticks in his head like a clock.

Echidna

I thought I'd buried her.
The malodorous scales
That made up her rotting tail
Had been planted in mud,
As if I expected to grow reptiles.

At least her voice is still.
The primal scream that rent the air
From behind her pointing finger;
The swinging sword of her harangue,
Has died in the pipe that played it.

Do you think that putting
The fleshy pieces back on her bones
You could build her more sweetly?
She is just as deadly, despite
Her uselessly mouldered cadaver.

Now it is her mephitic odour
That seeks places upon me, around me,
In the room, in the house,
To hang its commemoration of her
Like garlands of stinkhorn and iris.

You have up-dug the half-woman
And brought her back in as many pieces
As you found. Are you blind
To the dogs that follow?
It is time to put her back in the ground.

Dr Crippen

He thought, as he boarded the ship,
The vessel of his deliverance,
The conduit of his elusion, that his wife
Still lay where he left her,
Certified dead. But that

Was only the marriage certificate.
It blows in her fingers as she reads
And re-reads what he has done to her.
Her puzzled face has watched
His performance for years

And now sees nothing in his act
That loves her. Her poison
Is not so fast; she'll live through it,
Right up to his last breath,
Or hers.

The knowledge that the barb
Was tipped for her end, even as
Her husband took up the pen
In the church, is pursuing
The hyoscine in her bloodstream.

Crippen is escaping on water,
But truth is quicker now,
Fast as a shout and pregnant with disclosure.
His story has already arrived
And is waiting.

Nemesis

Nemesis is dressing for the party.
She wears her high red heels
And her red silk slacks, she hangs
A weight of gold chain at her belly
As a reminder of purpose.

Nemesis is innocent of the eyes
That follow her around the room,
Waiting to see whose musical chair
She removes,
Leaving them seatless.

Nemesis is introduced to no one
Whose pride belittles their physical body,
Until she meets the man
With his surname detached
As unnecessary.

Nemesis meets this single-storey identity
And asks him for identification,
Since his fame has not
Put his photograph
In front of her.

Nemesis sees his black irises
Like two pen-ends, inking him in,
Willing her to know him when
He could be Bloggs, or Smith, or Halibut
But his mouth remains shut.

Nemesis is left standing
As he turns his back, his fingers
Dismissing her, his first words being:
'It doesn't matter,
It doesn't matter.'

Nemesis is asked why. She replies:
'A man of no significance
Would classify himself
In order not to be
Otherwise mistaken.'

'A man of great importance
Would use his name
To point himself out
As having exceeded
His origins.'

'But a man who turns away
Because his epithet was not
Recognised in his features,
And says "it doesn't matter"
Describes himself.'

Sawney Beane

He likes people.
But it is only after their death
That the relationship really begins.

He chooses carefully,
Who to ask home for a meal.
He likes them to live long enough
For six or eight meetings,
He needs a number he can count on
To say they met 'often'. It is the word
He keeps dart-sharp,
Stropped on his hide.

He is still grafted like a stick
To the root of his lost look
At a would-be lover, left alone
To face devils he was too fearful for.
When they had ripped her to pieces
He found her more attractive,
And has been marrying her in his mind
Ever since.

The sharpened quill which he tore
From the head of her dead husband,
Is blunting beneath his balled fist
As it crosses the pages, scratching him in
To that other life as if
He had really lived in it.
Each rewrite makes a longer chapter of him.

Meetings that took minutes, or an hour,
Become days. His imagination, like a blind hand,
Fingers his conscience for boundaries
And finds none.

And this isn't the only body
He's got boiling.

Arachne

Young, she could tell tales in her embroidery
That the neighbours gagged over.
Not a writer by nature
She could still spin a yarn,
Drafted from fiction and picked out
Of the materials to hand
With the needle of her tongue.

Middling, she remained undiscovered,
But the death of a local woman
Made famous by the violence of her departure
Opened up the opportunity of kinship,
Of real friendship, if pressed. Arachne
Took out her silks and began to sew,
Stitching herself in.

Old, shrunken on her bones like an emptied shuttle,
She looked back at her tapestry.
Her thread was running thin,
She could see holes appearing where
Her stories had been fingered by questioning strangers,
And all of her invention; her stolen friend
Now unravelling.

And she, a spider.

Hera

Hera met her husband over dinner
At the house of his mistress.
So stricken was she to find herself
Outmatched, she fainted.

Until then, she had been unqueenly,
Her light was not best noticed
In the company of others. But this way
They were silenced.

Zeus had ignored her. Her youth
Had blinded him, but now
Her body found form beneath his fingers
As he carried her.

She knew she had him then,
As the bones of her spine
Inclined towards the sardius
Of his breastplate.

Even his mistress attended her,
And she saw what it was
To be made godlike
At his side.

She so convinced him that she
Was his well of compassion,
A mother for his infants,
And a custodian for his legacy,

That he made her his bride.
When she had settled in,
She set about the task
Of unhitching his children.

Pontius Pilate

Unsure that she acted from malice,
His mother is brought before him.
He's done Jesus,
His mother should be no matter.

His eyes swivel in his head,
Effacing her stare. Even when
She looks elsewhere, he can feel her
Burning like a poker in his heart's furnace.

She has kept things from him;
The land his father left, his birth-house
And father's face in photographs,
She has fenced them in with her sheep.

Should they escape, she says,
She would not eat, being poor in the sight
Of the king she would sit with,
At his right hand for as long as the memory

Of her husband's name remain attached.
Her son could sever it from her head
And put her right. Until now, her wrong has been
A thing he believed done to others.

As a child she was his landscape and succour,
Even when her winter descended,
Driving his father off into the blizzard
In which his body perished,

Leaving his son to grow accustomed
To the cold at his mother's breast.
And now his mother holds his birthright,
But still composes love notes to keep him.

Craving justice, he contrives
To cast blame from himself, so when
His sister calls upon the strength of God
In church, in judgement for sentence,

And God drives the ball of his fist through the roof,
Leaving his mother dead in the fallen debris,
She dies believing his hands innocent
Of the fingers that pointed her out,

Calling for water to wash in.

Prometheus

Every man depicts himself.
Prometheus, dangling from his chains
Is in performance even as
Prometheus dangles from his chains.

A ball ablaze in oil, swings from a crane,
Like a sun, across the face of Xerxes.
Prometheus watches himself, written in
To the play of himself,

In a borrowed tomb,
Having stolen fire,
As prisoner,
Liver eaten daily by

A liver-eater, replenished by gods
For the eagle to come again.
The audience sits out in the desert
On stones, and prays for Heracles

And an arrow to stop
The bloody eagle eating.
There is no one who isn't grateful
When the bird is butchered.

Prometheus watches Prometheus
Drag off a rock from his prison
Attached to a ring on his finger
As a reminder of the marriage.

Tomorrow the play will come again
But he,
He is still shackled to his mountain.

Honos

Honos is having a crisis of conscience.
Her probity, once priceless,
Now has a value.
It has weighed up against her virtue
Since she buried her husband.
A man of letters, his words
Were the clay that made him,
Even as God made man.
He stood,
Sculpted of his sentences.
Honos thought him thoughtless
For writing about anything
That reminded his readers
How she had not been
All there was.
So many of the words he left behind
Once handled in the furnace
Of his fireball,
Were leather-bound and limited
Only for private collectors.
Honos hears them at night
Screaming to be let out and read,
To honour the man that made them,
And remember him
In the minds of others.

Honos has not slept for three years.

But if the weight of her body
Can keep the books shut like mouths,
She will not have to face the sum of herself
Measured up against his feelings
For the people in them.

Lucrezia Borgia

She just can't keep it closed.
Every time her legs part
Her bearded mouth speaks. Its clitoral tongue
Can form words.

It tells of all the things it has seen,
Of all the places it has been,
Of all the phalluses
That have filled it.

Being young, she found no one
Listened to the hole in her head
Half as much as they answered the call
Of the hole between her legs.

Now her labia are releasing their secrets,
Her clitoris has dictated its memoirs
And made itself important.
She has known great men,

But only from the waist down.

Satan

I am the dilemma
In a man's mind. I shift
My body weight along the balance
Of his two thoughts, because man
Has two thoughts about everything,
And with every two thoughts

Come disadvantages. It's me
That weighs up the cost of conscience
Which scurries, furtive,
Around the inside of his cranium
Searching for a room
It can lock itself into.

Some men are born with guilt
Suckling at their breast, in need
Of drawing blood for a feed.
Others, have conscience nailed up tight,
Even before they are severed
From their mother's placenta.

They do what looks right, only
As long as someone's looking.
Their price is as low as a gutter-coin,
And a coin in the gutter will buy me
A whole death in some places,
In others, they do it for free.

I topple presidents. I am the weakness
That makes a man think
The secrets of his penis
Are impenetrable. I am the last drink
That unhooks the tongue
Of the one with the story.

I am the voice in the head
Of the woman who wants,
And wants and wants and feels
Badly done by if she doesn't get,
But hasn't found out
What it is she wants yet.

I am the seed from the soldier,
Worse than a bullet, when he has
Tied down his enemy's wife
And given her life, with his lips
On its little face, and his eyes
Begging for a breast

From the holes in its little head.
Better that it be born dead,
But he keeps her there
Till the brat be born squalling;
Every howl is mine,
The mother's most.

I am the cataract in the eye
Of their source of redemption,
Each man, each woman, blind
To the wailing, open wound of infant
Whose father bred it from the pit
Of all that makes him kill, and woman

Made mother against her will,
To carry, feed and grow the thing
That knows my name. I am
The question that the babes should die;
Because two days on earth and they are
Heading for hell, and I'm waiting.

Don't mistake me for a flood or a landslide,
Nor see me diseased and multiply
What man made. Nor am I fire;
I only felt inside the fingers of the boy
Who picked the matches up
And set alight the trees.

I'd bring him to his knees if he were mine,
Cupboard-shut and wailing for food
Until he's weak enough to listen
Next time. Someone already
Has a bath and a bin bag for the wet ones,
Tied up inside, stinking,

Waiting for morning in fear
At the first noise.
It's not my war when murder takes
God's name in vain. I'm only
Counting weaknesses. He needs to know
The worthlessness of souls;

The hollow rattle of the tin
That each one counts its cost in.
And when I have the sum
Of each of you, and you
Add up to nought,
My job is done.

The First Horseman

Behold a white horse, and he that sat on him had a bow; and a crown given unto him: and he went forth conquering, and to conquer. (REVELATIONS 6)

Tented women, denied even faces in daylight,
Or eyeholes lest a muddied iris
Cast a spell to topple a weakened man,
Stumble, legless in traffic,
Blinded by sweat and tears,
Oppressed by man's fear
That his penis be tempted.
And it might as well be a knife
If he not be her husband.

Man is set against woman
And makes her his enemy,
Woman is set against man
And makes him her enemy,
Even as the means of worship
Set God against God.
God against himself.

The disciples do not know
They are followers.
They think they are kings,
Having cut down, imprisoned, tortured
Or suppressed the opposition.
It would not occur to them to step up
On the box of their own great achievement,
And be offered a kingdom.

The first horseman is watching,
As mankind whittles itself down
To the last survivor,
Then he will dismount
And stamp them out like an insect,
Hang his crown
On the branch of a dead tree,
And go home.

The Second Horseman

And there went out another horse that was red: and power was given to him that sat thereon to take peace from the earth, and that they should kill one another: and there was given unto him a great sword. (REVELATIONS 6)

The horseman's sword bisects
A father's reason from belief.
Unfettered by thought,
His belief aspires
To become a reason in itself,
And he gives up his boy for it.

The boy bomber is strapped into his kill-suit;
He will go off, spectacularly.
Inside, all his little sons and daughters
Huddle their halves in his scrotum.

They would have opened like flowers
And bloomed, in a woman's womb.
They would have been the best he did,
If he did nothing else.

His father, having seen his son
Used as a weapon, is proud,
Himself now becoming
A dead end.

The Third Horseman

*And lo a black horse; and he that sat on him had a pair of balances
in his hand . . . a measure of wheat for a penny, three measures of barley
for a penny, see thee hurt not the oil and the wine.* (REVELATIONS 6)

I've measured 'em up. Each one's weight
Against the sum of their intention,
And found their intentions
Leave them lying useless in the bottom
Of the scale's cup.

Their barley and wheat is hybrid for seed
That could not put down a root
To source life and bloom,
Budding its nurselings
For the hungry to eat.

These kernels make bread, but planted,
Their thousands would rot before sprouting.
Voles and mice would carry off
The mildewed nuggets
But the grain be dead.

Man is made indispensable.
There's hardly a woman now,
Who won't be slit from hip to hip
To give her child an opening.
Nor a rose-shoot that will grow
From a fallen rose pip; this
Be no less reprehensible.

If nothing works without
The aid of interference, using tool
Or knife, or pill, to give a thing its life,
Then man be God, but less a God
Since breeding's been bred out.

The Fourth Horseman

Behold a pale horse: and his name that sat on him was Death,
and Hell followed with him. And power was given unto them over
the fourth part of the earth, to kill with sword, and with hunger,
and with death, and with the beasts of the earth. (REVELATIONS 6)

The cows are dead,
Bulldozed into pits
With a bullet in the head.

Sooty clod exhales balloons
Of blackened skin and burning hoof,
Nothing left for a handbag
Or a pair of shoes to put feet in.
Their stink beckons, their ghosts
Are windblown like chaff.

All their thousands of legs,
Stuck up from their barrels of bloat
And aiming at God, shout out:
'We're going this way,
We're going this way,
See us pointing pointlessly,
Here for no reason
And shot for blisters,
Not murdered for meat,
Nor poisonous to eat.'

The truck uplifts its trailer,
Hydraulics heaving, and into another burning bed
Tip woolly baubles. They bounce and roll
Until the last one comes to rest,
And from each tightly woollen fist
Falls a sheep's head.

And the farmer faces silence
From the furnace of his fields.
It hangs with the smoke
In the branches of his trees,
It hangs in each room of his house,
It hangs in his barn where the owls
Are speechless with horror, their voices
Gone out like candles.
It hangs from the rafters
Where he hangs.

The fourth horseman watches from
His pale mount. He has no time left
To carry out the offices of Death.
Far quicker then
To set man against the very thing
That feeds him.

Faust

Faust begged God
For an answer to everything, but God
Had his ears full from his houseful of souls,
Clamoured and weeping, with God, their pivot,
As their fault-handler and blame-holder.
God was busy.

Faust offered up to God his thoughts
On the origin of man, its euphony ascending
Like prayer. But God was already deafened.
The Devil, however, noticed Faust's
Unanswered oblation and watched
As Faust began to explore the *why* of things.

He used language to strip down artifice,
To open up the hidden mouth
In metal and earth, and the foetus
Dead at birth from a cow's belly,
And give them voice.
The Devil coveted such a soul

Who would go to all ends for an ending.
He bandaged and booted his cloven hooves
And presented himself. 'What,' he asked Faust,
'Would you most wish for,
If you could have it?'
Faust thought deeply. In his head
Was cradled his search
For the purpose of life, and the want,
Knock-knocking like a wooden cradle
Rocking the brass knob to the door
Through which, if he could only find it,
Would be the chamber of reason.

'I would give anything,' Faust replied,
'To know *why*.' The Devil laughed,
His own interest was *how*. 'For a soul
That is useless to you when you die,
The reason *why* shall be yours,' he cried,
And Faust found his eyes opened.

His world acquired the dimension of purpose.
Where others saw futility, he perceived
Necessity, where others saw stone, he saw
The volcano that spat it onto earth's anvil
To be made a pebble by water.
When others saw death, he saw

The soul, like a bell-sound,
Becoming pure in its passing
And ready for another time round,
Like a sword, fire tempered in the furnace,
Over and over, becoming better. And suddenly,
Faust knew he had been cheated.

The Devil sent a keeper as Faust's wife.
Now his work was over-watched, his words
Of working-out were stunted, since some
Were found offending and cut out.
His mind was governed by the mordant sound
Emanating from the crevice in

His wife's obdurate features.
Unsinned, he was driven to sin,
His understanding of it all
Made a prisoner of him. He saw,
As clearly as a shell in water, his wife
As a coldly handled daughter,

And her need to have her need be filled,
And filled and filled, as if the pit of her
Was endless to hell
Where all his efforts blazed, and where
He felt he was falling, too soon to know enough
Except the purchase of a soul was what

Those without, demanded most.
Without a soul, their curiosity extinct,
They felt nothing.
The Devil held out his hand
For Faust to topple into it, fresh
From the watch of his wife.

On leaving his body, Faust's soul resounded.
God heard the noise. It bore the weight
Of Faust's entire comprehension,
Except for an after-note, which sounded
As wrong as a dropped coin.
'You cannot take him!' God cried,

'He's incomplete, your bargain is undone.'
The Devil protested, but God was insistent
That Faust still lacked fulfilment. The Devil,
Aghast at being near enough to grasp
The thing he wanted, only now to lose it,
Cried out to Faust;

'You know birth, you know death,
You know the reason of us all.
What last unanswered question could be left?'
Faust, his soul, light on its feet and feeling
The loss of its prison at last, replied:
'I perceive the reason why

I could not be severed from
My pitied wife's remorseless care.
The thing that held me there,
Like some caught rat, faced with the meat
Of its own leg, between the tooth-trap
And freedom, was the very soul you want.

But for all the life in me
I cannot see, from the nothing that she is,
The purpose of her being.'
Faced with this impairment, this chip
In the honed surface of Faust's awakening,
The Devil was forced to set him free.

Lazarus

Sometimes, God is not enough.
When prayer cannot bring you back
From the pit of your cinders,
From the box at the bedside
In which you are crumbled,
To see what has been done
In your name, and that your children
Are kept from your pieces,
You must beg, dumb in death,
For the power of speech.

It could begin with a word; one of many.
Something written. Maybe that word
Will gather speed and momentum, it may even
Drag its brothers and sisters, its cousins, its aunts
And all their syllables and rise up
Like an echo in the mouth
Of the memory of you.
Maybe this new man,
Made up of your own mind
From the words you left behind,
Will read out your last letter

And make you heard.

Cerberus

Cerberus has guarded the truth for later.
He has seen it hidden
By those given hope for reconciliation
With the inventors and prevaricators.
But it doesn't come,
And the untruthful prosper
While the rest wait unwisely.
Just as pomegranates grow
From their myriad eyes,
He's tossing dragon's teeth to the ground
And sowing men.
The Spartoi rise up
From their dragon's root,
Their arms and legs new from the mud.
He is letting them go.
They will take the truth back from Hades
In their many mouths,
And set it free.

ABOUT THE CHARACTERS

Arachne: In Greek mythology Arachne was a Lydian girl, a weaver and embroiderer of unsurpassed skill, reputed to be a pupil of Athena though she vehemently denied it. When the goddess appeared to Arachne in the guise of an old woman, Arachne was rude and insulting despite the old woman's advice that she should be more modest. Arachne declared herself better than the goddess, who then revealed herself, prompting a contest between them. Arachne's work was so perfect that Athena tore it up in fury. Arachne lost heart and hanged herself but Athena wouldn't let her die and turned her into a spider.

Burke and Hare: William Burke (1792–1829) was born in County Tyrone, Ireland, moving to Scotland around 1818. In 1827 he was living with another Irishman, William Hare, who kept a boardinghouse in Edinburgh. At that time medical students and doctors were in desperate need of cadavers for dissection. When one of Hare's lodgers died, he and Burke sold the body to the anatomist Robert Knox. From then on, Burke and Hare with the help of Mrs Hare and Helen McDougal took to luring travellers. They plied them with drink and suffocated them, then sold the corpses. The disappearance of their 16th victim was noticed and police traced the body to Knox's cellar. Hare turned King's Evidence in order to convict Burke, who was hanged in Edinburgh on 28 January 1829. Hare was never prosecuted.

Cerberus: Cerberus was the dog chained at the gates of Hades who kept the dead in and the living out. He is sometimes described as having three dogs' heads, a serpent's tail, and snakes' heads sprouting from his back. He was thought to be the son of Echidna and Typhon. (The Spartoi in the poem 'Cerberus' were sown men who sprang up from the teeth of the dragon killed by Cadmus.)

Cinderella: A fable from Grimms' fairy tales, the details of this story are often misrepresented: the so-called ugly sisters are beautiful, being ugly only by nature, and they get their eyes picked out by birds at their stepsister's wedding to the prince. The basics, however, remain: Cinderella's mother dies and her father remarries. His new wife has two daughters who dislike their new sister so much, she is relegated to the kitchen to sleep in the ashes and work like a slave. When three-day festivities are announced to help the prince find a bride, Cinderella is forbidden to join her stepsisters. She has planted a branch, now a tree, on her mother's grave, and each day of the festivities she asks it for help and is given a dress to wear, each one more beautiful then the last. The prince only has eyes for her, but she escapes him each night to get back to her hearth. The third night he has had pitch pasted across the palace steps and Cinderella's golden shoe gets stuck in it. First one sister, then the other, is persuaded by her mother to cut a bit off her foot in order to fit the shoe and fool the prince. But the blood and tell-tale songs from the birds betray them. When at last Cinderella tries the shoe and it fits, he marries her and she is free.

Circe: In Greek mythology, the daughter of Helios and Perseis (or Hecate). Circe had the ability to change men into animals by touching them with a wand. She transformed Odysseus's crew into animals when they were sent to explore the island of Aeaea, where she lived. Odysseus persuaded her to free them by threatening her, having remained untouched by her spell after putting a magic plant called moly in the drink she gave him.

Crippen: Hawley Harvey Crippen (1862–1910) was hanged at Pentonville prison on 23 November 1910 for the murder of his wife, who went by the stage name of Belle Elmore, by poisoning with hyoscine. Crippen, an American citizen, moved to London with Belle in 1900. Three years before the murder, he started an affair with a typist, Ethel Le Neve. Mrs Crippen was last seen alive at a social function on the evening of 31 January 1910. Crippen let it be known that his wife had returned to the States on family business and later died of pneumonia. Eventually, suspicion as to Mrs Crippen's actual whereabouts prompted an investigation, which drove Crippen to return to America with Ethel Le Neve. Crippen's home was searched and human remains discovered beneath the cellar floor. Crippen and Ethel Le Neve were arrested onboard ship when the information was relayed by telegraph, the first apprehension of a suspect effected in this manner.

Damocles: A member of the court of the elder Dionysius of Syracuse (405–367 B.C.), Damocles was covetous of the pleasures enjoyed by his tyrant master, a man of wealth and success. Dionysius invited him to an extravagant banquet, where he found himself seated under a naked sword hanging from a single hair, symbolising the precariousness of the tyrant's fortune.

Durga: Durga was the wife of Siva, generally known as Kali (dark) or Kali Mai (dark mother) in Hindu mythology, a goddess of death and destruction. Usually black, she has four arms. Her eyes and the palms of her hands are red. Her tongue, face and breasts are bloodstained, her hair matted and her teeth like fangs. She wears a necklace of skulls, corpses for earrings and a girdle of snakes.

Echidna: In Greek mythology, a monster woman with a serpent's tail instead of legs.

Faust (Faustus): The name of a charlatan and erstwhile magician who died in 1540; there was a suggestion that two men used the name: Georgius and Johann. Faust was taken up by many authors as the representative black magician of his time. His posthumous fame, despite his ignoble history, was promoted in a book by an anonymous author, Faustbuch, published by Johann Spies in Frankfurt-on-Main in 1587, apparently using derivatives of many tales of sorcery from other sources which were newly attributed to Faust.

Christopher Marlowe's drama *The Tragicall History of Doctor Faustus* was first performed around 1592. The pursuit of knowledge, the involvement with black magic, and bargains made with the devil were all Faustian associations. In 1808, Goethe's *Faust*, part I, was published, with a promise of salvation in the prologue; *Faust*, part II, was published in 1833.

Four Horsemen: From Revelations (of St John the Divine), ch. 6. Upon the opening of the book of seven seals, the four horsemen are released to wreak death and vengeance upon the wicked people of the earth, while those marked by the seal of God on their foreheads are spared.

The First Horseman: He sits on a white horse; he was given a bow and a crown and sent forth to conquer.

The Second Horseman: He sits on a red horse; he was given a great sword and the power to take peace from the earth so that men would kill one another.

The Third Horseman: He sits on a black horse. He was given a set of scales – for the purpose of weighing the grain, for measuring.

The Fourth Horseman: He sits on a pale horse. He was given the power to kill with the sword, with starvation and with the beasts of the earth.

Hera: In Greek mythology, the Olympian goddess, daughter of Cronus and Rhea, and sister to Zeus, whom she married. Hera is often portrayed as vengeful and cruel; she used her gifts to torture and torment Zeus's mistresses and children.

Herse: In Greek mythology Herse (mentioned in the poem 'Madame Tussaud') was one of the three daughters of Cecrops and Aglaurus. Her sisters were Aglaurus and Pandrosus. Athena entrusted them with a basket containing the baby Erichthonius. She instructed the sisters not to open the basket, but they were curious and disobeyed. Athena punished Herse by sending her mad; she threw herself from the top of the Acropolis and died.

Hippolytus: In Greek legend Hippolytus was the son of Theseus and Hippolyte. His stepmother, Phaedra, fell in love with him, but he rejected her. Phaedra accused him of rape and his father called on Poseidon to kill him. Hippolytus was dragged to death when Poseidon sent a sea monster to terrify the horses as he drove his chariot by the sea. On hearing of his death, Phaedra hanged herself.

Honos: Honos was the Roman personification of morality, truth and virtue.

Houdini (1874–1926): Harry Houdini's real name was Ehrich Weiss. A Hungarian-born immigrant who lived his early years in Appleton, Wisconsin, USA, he began performing at 13, doing simple card tricks. He graduated to more and more spectacular stunts and became renowned for his abilities as an escape artist.

Jezebel: A name usually applied to a wicked, untrustworthy woman. In the Bible, Jezebel was daughter of Ethbaal, priest of Astarte (King of the Sidonians). She married Ahab, king of Israel. The prophet Elijah was instructed by God to curse Jezebel and Ahab, saying that she would be eaten by dogs and that Ahab would die, after Jezebel engineered the stoning to death of Naboth so that her husband could own Naboth's vineyard (I Kings 23). Following Ahab's death in battle against the king of Syria, Jezebel tried to replace the worship of Yahweh with that of the Tyrian Baal, Melkert. Jezebel and many of her Baal worshippers were put to death.

Job: A God-fearing man from the Bible (Book of Job) who was sorely tested by Satan, who sought leave from God to do so (Job 1.12). Job lost his animals, servants and children. He suffered such mental and physical pain that he wished for death. At last, having been cruelly tested by Satan in the sight of God without losing his faith or his honour, God restored double what Job had possessed before.

Judas: Judas Iscariot betrayed Jesus to the officers of the priests and Pharisees (John 18.1), resulting in Jesus's crucifixion.

Lady Macbeth: In Shakespeare's play Lady Macbeth persuaded her faltering husband to kill Duncan, king of Scotland, in order to take the throne. She implicated Duncan's drugged and sleeping grooms by smearing them with Duncan's blood from their own daggers when Macbeth himself could not go back to do this.

Lazarus: In the Bible (John 11) Lazarus is brother of Mary (who anointed Jesus's feet with oil and wiped them with her hair) and Martha. Jesus brought Lazarus back from the dead after four days.

Loki: In Norse legend, the god of mischief.

Lucrezia Borgia (1480–1519): Born of the Spanish cardinal Rodrigo Borgia (later pope Alexander VI) and his Roman mistress Vannozza dei Catanei. Lucrezia's father and brother Cesare used her, through several arranged marriages, as a political pawn.

Madame Tussaud (née Grosholtz) (1761-1850): Madame Tussaud's career as a waxwork maker began in the French revolution when she was asked to keep a record of the heads of the beheaded noblemen by constructing their likeness from wax. She later moved to London and continued her work until her last model, which was a life-size model of herself in 1842 at the age of 81.

Malchus: In the Bible (John 18.10), Malchus is described as servant to the high priest, who accompanied the men and officers sent by the chief priests and Pharisees to arrest Jesus in the garden of Gethsemane, prior to his crucifixion. The disciple Simon Peter cut off Malchus's ear with a sword.

Malvolio: As steward to Olivia in Shakespeare's *Twelfth Night*, Malvolio was duped by a forged letter purporting to be from Olivia, requesting that he wear certain clothing and behave in a particular manner, which in reality Olivia found offensive. It made him appear mad, and this was the sport.

Medea: In Greek legend Medea was the daughter of Aeetes, king of Colchis, and Idyia. (In some accounts Hecate was her mother.) Aeetes had imprisoned his daughter because she was opposed to his killing of all foreigners, but the day the Argonauts landed in Colchis she escaped and joined them. Medea gave Jason ointment to protect him from the bulls of Hephaestus, and sent the dragon to sleep in order that Jason might take possession of the Golden Fleece. In return, Jason promised to marry her. She even kidnapped and killed her brother, cutting him into pieces in an attempt to delay her father's pursuit of them.

Jason and Medea had two sons. They lived for a while in Corinth until Creon, king of Corinth, decided Jason should marry his daughter Creusa. He banished Medea but she obtained a day's delay. She took this opportunity to send a poisoned dress and ornaments to Creusa. When Creusa put them on she died from mysterious burns, as did her father, who tried to help her. Medea then killed her own children in an effort to cause Jason as much anguish as she could in a form of punishment, before fleeing to Athens.

Medusa: One of three Gorgons. Medusa was mortal, her sisters were immortal. Their heads were massed with snakes and one glance at them would turn a person to stone.

Merlin: Merlin is the magician from the legends of King Arthur who protects and advises him.

Morgan Le Fey: Fairy half-sister to king Arthur, possessed of magical abilities. There are numerous versions of Morgan's part in the Arthurian legends. She was generally considered to have been Merlin's adversary and author of King Arthur's downfall through her son, Mordred. In some versions of the legend Merlin fell in love with and was magically imprisoned by Morgan, in others, it was Vivian, Lady of the Lake, who imprisoned him, having learned all she could of his magic.

Narcissus: In Greek mythology, son of the river-god Cephissus and the nymph Leiriope, he was acknowledged for his beauty. The seer Tiresias told his mother that he would live long if he never saw his own reflection. Narcissus's rejection of the nymph Echo was supposed to have been the cause of her wasting away until nothing was left but her voice. The gods became angry and arranged that he should catch sight of himself in a stream. He could not tear himself away from the vision of his own beauty and died there. A narcissus grew on the spot. (Alternative version: Ameinias is in love with Narcissus and Narcissus sends him a sword. Ameinias kills himself with it, cursing Narcissus as he does so.)

Nebuchadnezzar: Nebuchadnezzar was the Babylonian king who built a colossal golden image which he demanded the many nations and peoples over whom he ruled should worship (described in the Bible, Daniel 3). Three men—Shadrach, Meshach and Abednego—refused to worship the effigy and were thrown into a burning furnace. They emerged unscathed, protected by God, and Nebuchadnezzar decreed that no one should in future denounce their god.

Nemesis: The goddess Nemesis was one of the daughters of Nyx and was much loved by Zeus, who pursued her. She was the goddess of the punishment of crime, also responsible for the curbing of excessive good fortune, bragging and pride.

Pandora: In Greek myth, Pandora was created by Hephaestus and Athena at Zeus's request as punishment for the human race to whom Prometheus had just given fire. Once on earth Pandora lifted the lid of a pot (or box), which released all the evils on the world. Hope was the last thing left inside, but Pandora trapped it when she replaced the lid.

Pontius Pilate: Pilate called for water to wash his hands of the decision to crucify Jesus, saying as he did so 'His blood be on us, and on our children' (Matthew 27.1). He allowed the mob to have their way and released Barabbas instead, refusing to take responsibility for his actions.

Prometheus: In Greek mythology Prometheus was the son of the Titan Iapetus. His mother was Asia, daughter of Oceanus, or the sea nymph Clymene. There are variations in the legends in which Prometheus features. Some describe him as being the creator of the first men, making them from clay, in others he is simply a benefactor to mankind. He brought down the wrath of Zeus on man by dividing a bull for sacrifice. He wrapped the meat and intestines in the skin, topped off with the stomach, then wrapped the bones in the fat. Zeus was asked to choose his sacrifice and chose the pile of bones and fat. As punishment, Zeus withheld fire from mortals, but Prometheus stole fire in a fennel stalk (the legends vary). Zeus had Prometheus chained to a rock in the Caucasus and sent an eagle born of Typhon and Echidna to eat his liver daily, and daily, his liver would regenerate. Heracles, son of Zeus, shot the eagle, releasing Prometheus. Zeus then forced Prometheus to wear a ring made from his chains to which was attached a piece of the rock he had been anchored to.

Rasputin: Gregory Efimovitch Rasputin (1871–1916) was a Russian monk born in the village of Pokrovskoe. He devoted himself to religion, declaring that he was inspired by God. His passionate nature and considerable physical strength added effect to his religious fervour. He adopted the beliefs of a sect known as the Khlystry, a central belief being that salvation could only be achieved through repentance. His interpretation of this was: 'Sin in order that you may obtain forgiveness.'

He travelled and studied and was eventually introduced to the empress, who believed him to have a beneficial effect on the haemophilia suffered by her son, which won him tremendous influence at court and allowed him to ensure the appointment of the most unlikely people to high offices. His popularity and abuse of power led to his assassination on 16 December 1916 when the Grand Duke Dimitri Pavlovich, Prince Yussupoff and Purichkevich invited him to supper at the Yussupoff Palace. Potassium cyanide put in his wine failed to kill him, so they shot him dead.

Romulus and Remus: In Roman mythology, Numitor, king of Alba Longa, was deposed by his younger brother Amulius. Numitor's daughter Rhea Silva gave birth to twins, claiming the god Mars was their father, but Amulius ordered them thrown into the Tiber to drown. The trough (or basket) in which they floated came to rest at the site upon which Rome was built. Here, they were nurtured by a she-wolf and a woodpecker. They were later found and brought up by Faustulus and his wife. Eventually, they were recognised as the grandsons of Numitor, killed their great-uncle and restored their grandfather to the throne. They founded the city of Rome. Romulus killed his brother for leaping the wall he had built around the city as an example to others who would try it.

Rumpelstiltskin: From Grimms' fairy tales: A miller, in an effort to attract the attention of the king, boasted that his daughter could spin gold from straw. The king locked her in a room to prove the claim, on pain of death. Rumpelstiltskin appeared and spun the straw into gold in return for her necklace. The following night, the girl was forced to perform the same task on a bigger room full of straw and Rumpelstiltskin saved her in return for her ring. On the third night the girl was made to perform the same feat with a yet bigger room of straw and in return she would become queen. This time the girl was forced to promise Rumpelstiltskin her first child, as she had nothing left with which to repay him for his help. She was duly made queen and Rumpelstiltskin came to collect his prize when she gave birth. At her protests, he finally agreed to give her three days to find out his name, in which case she could keep the child. He was overheard, dancing around a fire, boasting about his name. When he came to the queen and she was able to tell him what it was, he was so incensed that he stamped his right foot into the ground, then pulled at his left foot in an attempt to free himself, splitting himself in two.

Salome: Salome is said in the Bible to be daughter of the disinherited Herod Philip and Herodias. Her mother, Herodias, later married Herod Antipas, for whom Salome danced so beautifully that he offered her anything she asked for, up to half his kingdom. Salome consulted her mother. Herodias feared John the Baptist, who was being held in jail, because he maintained she should not have married her husband's brother, so she instructed her daughter to ask for his head. Having given his word, Herod could not now go back on it. John was beheaded and his head presented to Salome.

Samson: In Hebrew folk legend (and the Bible, Judges 14–16) Samson belonged to the tribe of Dan and was renowned for his actions against the Philistines. He fell in love with Delilah, who was persuaded by the Philistines to discover the root of Samson's strength. Three times he lied to her, but the fourth time he gave in to her pleas and confessed that his strength was in his hair. He fell asleep in her lap and she cut his hair. Weakened, the Philistines were able to capture and blind him. They kept him prisoner until the day they tied him between two pillars of a house to make sport of him. His hair had been growing and his strength had returned enough to pull out the pillars and kill everyone in the building, including himself.

Sawney Beane: A cannibalistic Scotsman (from the time of the Calvinists) who waylaid travellers to rob and eat them. He was only discovered when one of the victims escaped and led soldiers back to search for his attacker. Sawney Beane and his woman had interbred a family of many. They were found amongst piles of body parts which were being cured, and the money, jewellery, weapons and clothes of their victims.

Sibyl: Sibyl, daughter of Zeus and Lamia, was a prophetess. Sibyl became the name given to all those gifted with the ability to

93

prophecy. Another Sibyl was Herophile, a native of Marpessus in the Troad.

Simeon: In the Bible (Luke 2.25) Simeon is the second son of Jacob, ancestor of one of the twelve tribes. It was revealed to Simeon by the Holy Ghost that he would not die until he had seen Christ. The Spirit led him to the temple at the time Jesus's parents brought him there. He blessed Jesus and divulged that Jesus was the sign which was awaited, then he asked God to be allowed to depart in peace and die.

Sisyphus: In Greek mythology he was the son of Aeolus. He founded Corinth (then called Ephyra) and fathered Odysseus. Eventually he was condemned to the Underworld by Zeus, for exposing Zeus as kidnapper of Aegina. There, his perpetual task was to roll an enormous stone up a hill, only to see it roll down again, forever and ever. Some suppose the task was designed to keep him from finding a way to escape, because he had no time for anything else.

Sweeney Todd: A Victorian barber who recycled his customers by slitting their throats and tipping them into his cellar, where they became meat pies for his pie shop. He was exposed by the discovery of a fingernail in one of the pies.

Theramene: A friend of Phaedra's stepson Hippolytus (mentioned in the poem 'Hippolytus').

Thor: Norse god of thunder, son of Odin. Benevolent to humans. Depicted as middle-aged man of incredible strength.

Vlad the Impaler: Vlad III (1431–76) was the ruler of Wallachia, now part of modern Romania. He was known as Dracula, meaning son of the dragon or devil, and was finally assassinated. Somewhere in the region of 40,000 to 100,000 men, women and children were killed on his orders. His favoured method was impalement.